Learn Italian
Alphabets & Numbers

Published By: AuthorUnlock.com

ISBN-10: 1981204555

ISBN-13: 978-1981204557

A

Albero

Tree

B

Banana

Banana

C

Cane

Dog

D

Dadi

Dice

E

Elefante

Elephant

F

Fiore

Flower

G

Gatto

Cat

H

Hotel

Hotel

I

Imbuto

Funnel

L

Leone

Lion

M

Mela

Apple

N

Nave

Ship

Orologio

Clock

P

Pera

Pear

Q

Quadro

Painting

R

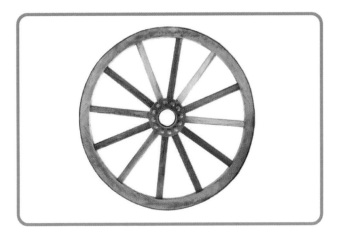

Ruota

Wheel

S

Sole

Sun

T

Tavolo

Table

U

Uva

Grapes

V

Vaso

Vase

Z

Zebra

Zebra

J

Jeans

Jeans

K

Koala

Koala (Bear)

W

Walkie Talkie

Walkie Talkie

X

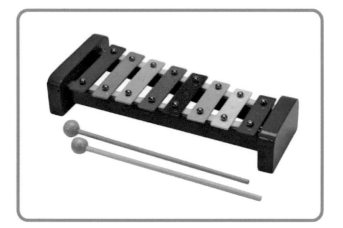

Xilofono

Xylophone

Y

Yacht

Yacht

0 - 10

Numbers

0 - 10

0

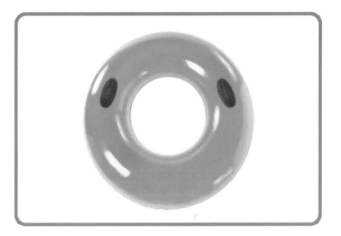

Zero

Zero

1

Uno

One

2

Due

Two

3

Tre

Three

4

Quattro

Four

5

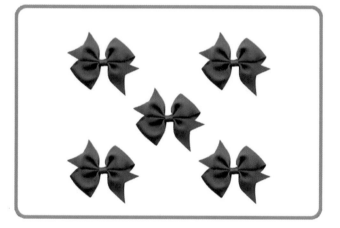

Cinque

Five

6

Sei

Six

7

Sette

Seven

8

Otto

Eight

9

Nove

Nine

10

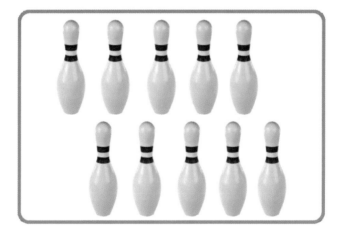

Dieci

Ten

Printed in Great Britain
by Amazon